burntdistrict

a journal of contemporary poetry

burntdistrict

a journal of contemporary poetry

Editors
Liz Kay & Jen Lambert

Volume 3 Issue 2
Summer 2014

Omaha, NE

TABLE OF CONTENTS

TABLE OF CONTENTS

TABLE OF CONTENTS

TABLE OF CONTENTS

LILLIAN KWOK

Le Carnaval Des Animaux: Le Cygne

We wake up very late, I pull your arm over my body and we sink back into sleep.
This is the last day of our lives so we can do whatever we want. This is what I want.
I want you always, but always means less than nothing to me. Let's paint our bodies
white and roll around on the dark roof so the gods will know that we were here.

Lillian Kwok

Le Carnaval Des Animaux VII: Aquarium

You are not a river, it disappoints me. You are incapable of drowning me, flooding your shores, turning my skin blue. I can't drink you from my two hands. For a while though, we were happy, swimming in the water, your hands in my hair, my legs around your waist. But now I'm on the rocks watching you swim, and I don't care if you stay there underwater, if you never come up again.

Margot

Midnight on Route 11. The bank sign flashes 32 degrees and as I shamble down the sidewalk I can't tell where my breath meets the dark. In Kauai, Margot is licking lips wet with whiskey and watching the surf hit the sand. She's wondering how stars can look so close when worlds stretch the distance between. Margot says she touches herself in the bathroom and thinks of me. I want to believe her. Alone outside the hardware store, I'm loathing the cornfields and waves—the miles between me and the small hairs on her thighs. My knuckles burn. The freeway murmurs its cheap river song, and the frost mocks the clouds in the sky. In the photos, Margot and I are laughing, sipping cheap wine and flirting through cigarettes and fog. We're each waiting for the other to look away. But they're only photos. Nobody's looking now.

During Lunch Break Paula Asks If I Love You

"Life is complicated but wonderful," she says between spoonfuls of African peanut soup. We sit on the bench by the gallery hugging the spicy paper cups until they are empty and we are warmer or less aware of wanting. That night on the stairs, my silences in your mouth, she must have seen your fingers noosed around the wine bottle and she wants me now to describe the bruises.

I am in love with her blueberry hair, how moths hunt it out of her dimples. She knows the morning weight of your door, your window's striped mouth, the Salgado album anchoring dust under your bed.

It was her birthday. How could you? There was sand on your sheets pressing its tiny ache to our hipbones.

Up on Commercial Street, the neighbor's black lab is flat against the asphalt, her tongue pointing east. She waits for the UPS truck because the driver might have treats. Dogs don't know what we know about giving up.

And you, I brought you almond biscotti once. We dipped them in whiskey, fell asleep on the couch. In my dream I was a school of hyacinth fish swimming inside the grand piano. In the morning the sun was draped on the laundry line.

Revere Beach

Things that evaporate:
boys, water.

In the end we stay
for the fireworks: skyfuls of Technicolor popcorn,
the plastic laughter of children
on the beach
one after another.
While everyone looks up
I lick my shoulder.

The waves at night are an echo
of our failures.
I collect beach glass bled dry.
The tide returns
a dead seagull.

Things that taste like salt:
boys, water.

I swim slowly
and the only way I can tell
where the ocean begins
and the sky ends
is that there is more moon in the ocean,
a lemon stain I push my arms through
until my teeth chatter,
a private explosion.
Goosebumps is how the body
mourns sunlight.

California Crows

i.

In my subconscious, the Donner Lake overflows,
and countless water-damaged, green-tinted molars
rise to its surface, like fish that have died
terrible deaths. My grandmother has told me before
that dreams involving teeth symbolize insecurity.

ii.

Here is what I know about Donner Lake:

It's in Northeastern California, close to the Sierra Nevada
and Lake Tahoe. Once, it was called "Truckee"— once,
before 39 lost pioneers died in front of the lake's shore
in a nineteenth century winter.

When all the veins in all 39 bodies had frozen like icicles,
the palest of the dead were separated, limb by limb,
and cured over a wheezing fire to feed the surviving members
of the catastrophic Donner Party.

Forty eight pioneers were rescued from the Sierra Nevada
in February 1847. Later, they found grisly bones
buried in the snow, with the carcasses of dormant grandfather clocks
and split butter churns.

iii.

I've only read about Donner Lake and its surrounding areas—
Donner Hill, Donner Pass, Donner Memorial State Park.
Other wagon trains traveling west in the mid-1800's took that area
as the bad omen you could not avoid, the crow that never left its perch.

iv.

I can hear the ominous caws of death feasting even
when I am awake. My mother wants to tape cotton
down to my bleeding gums. The marshy teeth

are separating themselves from their home in the water
when I wake up. I am a walking toothache,
chips of ivory on fire.

Every interpretation is "insecurity", as though that
did not already burst through my body
like an inevitable volcano explosion. No, I am not
a little toothache, I figure out. I am Pompeii reborn.

v.

Once, I could talk about death, finality, the tall black gown.
I see a quiet dentist on a Tuesday who tells me
that my jaw is never going to recover from the neglect
I put it against. I close my fists,
and picture the one-hundred-and-sixty-eight-year-old teeth
between California and Nevada fading into rotting dust.

I cannot blame insecurity anymore. Once, I could talk
about death. Once, I could talk.

Rebecca Connors

This is how to read me

Start left to right, keep
your eyes cross-haired
on my lines. Knock your teeth
against my consonants, my hardhearted
shell. Yesterday,
under haunted elms,
I found myself
detoured in the foothills –

found myself outside
your house. I will remind you
of the last time we crumbled
pecan pie, your fingers, absentminded,
rubbing my thigh.
Read me. Closer, I will
remind you of the tucked-hair
kisses. Serif-bound now,

I'm your ache in written words.
Keep your eyes on me as we move
to the next line, as we slide to the
last time. Use my hip as a guide
until you find us parting
on the highway, a handshake
at the gas station, receding
to smaller versions
of ourselves

1973

That was the year I looked down and saw frog
    bones jutting from the open tops of my toes. By which
        I mean I learned how to jump when needed. We all

steal the dead's muscle memory. By which I mean
    I flinch even when men who are not my grandfather
        salute the flag too quickly. It wasn't his fault. Vietnam

LSD, experiments in forever tracking the red
    shadows of what could not be shot. That year, summer
        was sneaking into the break between bank

and rapids, was interrogating
    surly sixth graders about war's secret
        plans. We knew blood, the intimate ways

of the body, by which I mean like toy
    planes. We knew how to leap
        off the curbs into our own

Mekong deltas, Chicago swarmed over
    with a wildness of rice. My first shot
        when I was eight, by which I mean my father

threw a knife across the room
    and then offered me a drink.
        My mother had turned the kitchen to a war,

the flour jar broken against the sink. Everything
    rising. We sat like a poor-
        boy's planes after that, trembling for the flight,

all cobbled together from what wings we could find.

Water Cycle #12: Afterlight

I want to die
as artfully as one glass of water
covers seven city blocks as fog.
The lungfish can live out of water
as long as four years & this cheers me
or at least leaves me
torn by tornadoes—the roofs, the trees,
a wooden horse explodes inside my house.
Meanwhile, the news turns off
so slowly you can watch it expire
into creosote & when I die you should
bury me into diamond.
Memory is just
another house. So much depends
on wires. To the dry season
its silos, its soft sag of cloud. They are thirsty.
They are thirsty. After the rain
a pornography of worms gathers
on the sidewalk. & after the clouds
sprawls a tarp of light, but it is not the same
light it was before the clouds.
This is how I would like to evolve.

Water Cycle #13: The Trees Sent Us Letters

That's how you know they mean what they say:
when it's written on their skin. We can't read
them, for the most part, just webs of ruddy rings
intersecting. But they keep coming,

stuffed in the mailbox at sunset, a clear effort
to confess—
what is it they want in whittling themselves away?
The thin forest reads over our shoulders,

hopeful. For our part, we unfold the sylvan calligraphy,
press it against the porch table & spend our eyes
on these rings that move through each other
like Sunday paper games—but it's not a game;

they've cut themselves to saplings, the forest
floor fresh with dust. How could they
give themselves to us like this? How could we
be so dumb? In the end we hang

the tapestry of letters on the windows
where the light lifts them, still unable
to make the most basic meanings, the house
ringed by wind.

MOLLY SUTTON KIEFER

Out of Sequence (Or, A Second Surgery)

[1]

Buttons of snow froth down. *How committed are you*
to this earth? On the way to the appointment, I do not see
the chameleon-car; I do not stop at the first sounds of metallic protest.
My car corners my mother's, bullies it in the driveway.
Crumples and outwinks its light.

Black crows burst from my chest. A decade ago, her fury
would bring down the four corners of our house.
Before I confess, I almost ask for my daughter back,
to hold her in my arms before my mother can think to use her as a weapon.

My mother holds me close, the three of us pressed in the kitchen,
she whispers to me about her brother, her father, both lost
in the time it takes for Maya to turn three months old,
her own bullied early retirement,
how her car's corner is *nothing.* She holds tighter.

Still, I can only think of one word as the tech's sticky baton wanders
over my jellied stomach: *menace.* There is no baby in there.
This ultrasound finds what it was looking for:
several stones, one exceptionally large.

[2]

In the surgery waiting room,
enticing our daughter to nap, he tells her, *When you wake up,*
maybe Mommy won't have that weird hat on.

[3]

And I don't even like babies—the nurse beckons other nurses in,
somehow my baby has become a magnet and she grins up
wildly at each blue ghost who says hello. The nurse covers my ears
with tape in the places the earrings won't come out, tells me

they cauterize the wound and wouldn't want to spark.
My wedding rings are back in a plastic bag.

I shuck all of my clothing, all but my nursing bra.
I wear a purple paper gown. There are slits,
enough for my flaccid breasts to peek through at the center,
a feeding before surgery. We grow sodden.

[4]

Some mornings, I find myself in balasana—child's pose—my cheek
gathering carpet lint, my daughter's legs bicycling in the bed above.
It feels as strong as a contraction, only no count in between.
Just a steady filling of air, a stretching and elbowing of organs,
the words throwing up and routine like a sweater set.

[5]

I'm on the table again, only how can anyone call this a table?
A body's outline, a sacrificial cross—the place convicts settle before
injection. I was led to this room as one might lead a dog, the leash
an IV bag; I am allowed to pause and mark a room as my own.
Rooms with televisions on spark notes about a royal wedding,
scrutinize the lace of a dress; my hands pinch back the purple
crepe between my nakedness and the world. The nurse chides me
about modesty. *This room is always so cold*, I tell them.
The radio plays Bad Company, and I think of how my best friend
stood in the hallway before the birth as they cracked me open,
my mother and father upstairs, sharing a newspaper—and this time,
they'll pull an organ through my belly button,
which is not how babies are born, after all,
but how the aftermath is tidied up.

And Life Goes On As It Has Always Gone On

Snow and then more of it and just when spring
seems possible, a blizzard leaves you powerless.
Your flowers in bud expire.
Something hurts your heart—an odd balloon
in your chest, poofing and unpoofing,
days in the hospital hooked up to machines,
then a diet stripped of cakes and pies.
Children ring your doorbell and disappear.
Late at night, when you can't sleep, the TV asks,
Do you know where your children are?
and you say, *No,* or *Yes, in jail.*
Bees build nests under the eaves of your house.
They hunt you down and stab you many times
with their tiny switchblades—even your lips
while you're eating a ham sandwich.
Blinded by an armful of fresh towels, you fall
down the stairs while rushing to answer the phone.
Your vertebrae shattered, that call from your lover
forever unanswered, sex forever impossible.
In Greece poppies cover the islands in spring,
scarlet flowers waving like silk scarves.
People in *kouzinas* eat poppy seed cakes
and speak of Demeter, how she devoured
the black seeds to fall asleep and forget
her grief over the loss of her daughter.
Outside your window, spring arrives flowerless.
Crackheads move in next door.
Your dog dies from a poisoned meatball.
Are you looking for compensation?
A rabbit nibbling the grass—does that console?
Does ice cream suffice? even if served
with marshmallow fluff? Delicious, but is it enough
as you lie in your hospital bed plugged to a monitor
and dreaming of sex, the little red pumping
machine of your heart opening like a poppy in bloom?

Nandini Dhar

Dream Collection

Long before we became twins and sisters, we were dolls—carved in our mother's noonday dreams. There wasn't any god. There wasn't any Sabbath. There wasn't even any goddess carving words of silt and kiln.

There were new leaves–one or two–in the pumpkin vine right outside the window. Thin as cellophane. So wan that light passed through. Raindrops on the tips: illuminated candles on leaves. A porch with Deepaboli lights. Only it was not Kali pujo. The bare branches: tweeting sparrows.

On the barnished wood of the dresser, colors of a rainbow. Two mother-hands carving little girls: seven of them. Each a color of the rainbow. Our mother, five-and-a-half months heavy: dreamt. Dreamt. And chewed on a guava: green as a parrot's plumes. She hated the rains, loved the rainbows. And dolls: porcelain, plastic. Pretty as the Murphy baby. Pretty as the mannequins in the children's clothing store. Delicate as the painting of a painting of a little child.

Long before we became twins and sisters, we were dolls—sculpted meticulous in our mother's noonday dreams. A premonition, a fantasy: of forever holding within one's fingers the tides of generations, one's own breed. A premonition, a fantasy: of forever knowing there is nothing outside of what the mother's fingers could touch.

The skin: the right shade of butter. Or the right shade of tree bark. The skirt, pressed tight. A corset shaped like a peacock tail. Hair, neatly brushed and ponytailed in purple love-in-Tokyo.Ten fingers, ten toes: perfect, nails clipped, polished. Big enough like a real baby, covering the entire length of your arm. Small enough to play with. Just like dolls.

Long before we became twins and sisters, we were dolls—carved in our mother's dusk-time dreams. Our mother dreams of all the dolls she would buy for us. Dragged them from the stores across four rail-stations. If the need be. A prayer in her voice: a delicate little nose, hair yellow enough to hold the sunlight. A face with baby chubs. *Oh god, please ignore my prayer.*

Baby-dolls tangled in the clothesline. Our mother dreamt of smelling sun in our hair. Our hairs tangled in the guava seeds. Mother spat them out.

Nandini Dhar

We were caught—in the motion of her hands pressing and folding doll-sized clothes. Our mother's dreams folded us like dolls into rumpled lace, paper-fan. Our mother etched little girls with her fingers on the sandpaper. Little girls with wings. Little girls in pink. Against a backdrop of half-moon and crooning stars.

Nandini Dhar

A Broken Fairytale

A horse the size of our teacher's chair in the bush by the canal. Its wings caught in the branches—flapping. My sister Tombur tried to ride its back, and it shook her off. The way one shook off the housefly of one's wrist. My sister pulled herself up, and we sat right outside the bush, laughing the counting the teeth of the horse. While it struggled to free itself. In the distance, most of the neighborhood boys were galloping away. Others rode the kites and crossed the canal. Tombur and I sat counting the horse's teeth. We did not know what to say to each other: we knew each other by heart. The canal water the color of moonless night, did not reflect the sky back.

Because we could not fill each others' silences, we held between our fingers, two broomsticks. One for each one of us. Rama and Ravana. Buddhu and Bhutum. Neither of us ever learnt the meaning of fidelity in stories. The epics were just some starting points. Nothing more. Nothing less. We made these princes go to school with us. We set them to illustrate our hometown with snot. And, when they failed, we punished. Without any mercy.

Neither of us waneds to be a princess. In the books Tombur read to me at night, the princesses hardly possessed a line. The princesses did not swirl their canoes anywhere. They did not have bows slinging across their backs. They did not sharpen the arrow-tips, let alone aiming them anywhere. They slept. Didn't do much else.

Because neither Tombur nor I could fill each others' silences, we wanted to break underfoot the barren repetition of memories. We wanted to do things. Rama did things. Ravana did things. Were therefore protagonists. We did away with the princesses. In the new play Tombur was writing, I was to be the rainbow. And it's easy. All I had to do was to wear a rainbow suit and do a bridge on stage. *Byas.*

This Town A Broken Glass Bangle

Our grandfathers did not write this city. Nor did our fathers. Or uncles. Neither did the city write itself. All they could do was to read it. As if it's an incomplete tableau. Afraid. That their touch would shatter the city like an old beetle wing. Afraid. They settled for a series of pragmatic magic instead. A broken line on a broken wall. Rhythms made unrhythmic through repetitions. Clay birds sculpted into molds. Molds re-sculpted into clay birds. They made clouds out of old ripped shirts, but did not have the courage to hang them on poles. When Tombur and I walked into the crevices of this city's shoulder bones, we did so with the tentativeness of their guilt. Like a gash from an axe. Lustrous red. A reminder. Not yet ten, and we learnt this was the price you pay when you try to step in to the footprints left by fathers.

From our porch to the rail station, the town was a broken glass bangle. Sharp on the edges, warped, a rickety rainbow inside. That house was too small for the two of us. Besides, Tombur never learnt to look properly under the bed. Or slip her fingers in between the cracks of the beds for little knick-knacks we got as gifts – empty match boxes, thumb-sized plastic dolls, whistles, plastic sun-glasses with thick blue borders. What was lost was lost. A street was different. Did not demand the touch of your fingers, the meticulousness of sweeping something clean, folding and being folded into neatness, pressed and ironed into folds. I could not gather these streets in between my fingers. Tombur said, gathering was what she was doing in everything she wrote and drew. That encyclopadia of ghosts, fairies, elves, aliens and princesses. These patterns she drew and re-drew. But she was not moving any closer. A form of learning lines by heart it was: this gathering. Memorizing, yet Tombur kept forgetting her lines. We did not ever have a falling-out, Tombur and I, because I did not tell her she was messing up the lines. Drawing them too thick and thin. That was why, she needed to draw and re-draw. Write and re-write. Could not get it quite right. I did not tell her that. But helped her to tear up the deficient ones.

Playing History House
after Gabrielle Calvocoressi and Arundhati Roy

Uncle so and so taught us that game. He wasn't a blood uncle. But then, no
one was. And we didn't care. Blood is the red thing that oozes out when you
accidentally pierce a finger while sharpening pencils. We did not want any
uncle-shaped tableaus in our blood. And, the real uncles are the ones who fill
you up with useless. *Anyways, that's not what I was trying to say.* Uncle so and
so taught us that game and we played it. Often. *Someone writes a word with the
tip of one's fingers on someone else's bare back and then you cover your eyes with
your hands and count ten and then you stop for a second and make a guess.* My
sister Tombur and I play that game with each other. Often. We begin with easy
ones. Like *poopoo.* I figure it out and say the word out loud. Then we shout out
the word to every corner of our terrace until our voices crack and we giggle a lot.
When it's my turn, I write *bastard.* We nibble at each others' heat rashes, popping
them with our nails. These letters, etching through the sweat of our skin, daring
us to peel off prohibitions: layer after layer. One by one. This was not what uncle
so and so had taught us. He used common words. But we do it differently. We try
fuck, fag, sisterfucker and *asshole.* No one here on this terrace to slap our cheeks.
No father. No mother. No aunt. No uncle. And then Tombur sits up. Takes a deep
breath, and scribbles, "Bimalkaku." Although we have never met him. He died.
Shot. In the swamps. Before we were born. We call him "kaku" anyway. And
we often played Bimalkaku-police amongst ourselves. One of us runs around
the terrace and then makes a face and falls along the walls. The walls are our
alleyways. Just like Mrinal Sen's films. But we don't anymore. Because Tombur,
who always has to be the spoil-sport, asked one day, were there any alleyways
and walls in the swamp where Bimalkaku was shot. None of us knew about that.
Anyway, that's not what I was trying to say. What it is, I write back, "Naxalbari."
Tombur shakes me by the shoulders and yells, "That's not a bad word." I didn't
know that. In their home, Bimalkaku's brothers do not hang his picture on the
wall. Like they do of those others who are also dead.

NANDINI DHAR

Independence Day, 1985

The morning of fifteenth August, 1985: the branches of the banyan trees, warped as broken bones, spitting out fishbones—white as ghost skin. National anthem in the school-yard, fingers in the cracks of the harmonium keys, a song that could have had a different plot. My sister Tombur confused the words she was taught, and began to sing the *Internationale* instead of the national anthem, and when slapped and asked for an explanation, said, *isn't that the you also have to stand up to sing?* It's true those were the only two songs that we knew that needed standing up to be sung. And Ria didn't memorize the notes well enough to sing without the notebook held in front, and Nilesh couldn't keep up with the rhythm on his tabla, and got it all mixed up in the middle and Kushal wouldn't cut out the heads of the father of the nation into neat little stick figures and no teacher would take the blame for these kids who had not learnt to become silver birds around the icing flowers in a strawberry-flavored cake. Of course, none of these children had ever seen a strawberry and think *strawberries* and *cherries* are the same thing – interchangeable. But they were neither ready to sing nor shimmer.

And there were shadows in that picture: the photographer shouting *esmile*, of the supposition that we're all to smile together, of posing there in the school-yard, of navy blue pleated skirt-tunics, navy blue trousers and starched white shirts, of the shortest ones sitting up front with the teachers, of slightly taller ones standing in the back.

We were seven and Tombur was scowling. Although she had been warned by our grandmother, right before leaving home: there were juju-ladies up in the mango tree in the school-yard. Who sucked the blood out of little girls who did not smile when asked to by the teachers. But my sister went around the neighborhood with her dress rolled up around the waist. She slapped others when slapped. Bit when called *ma*: beginning to figure out fingers can cause pain. There was a team there, in that school-yard, however broken. Her navy blue tunic crumpled, my sister would not play for it.

Thomas Cook

Overture in the Italian Style

Even Franz Schubert can do it this way. As the poet said, "I contradict my surname, even when it hearkens a dessert." The German strings and laces are brilliant, the Italian leather is brilliant, the Kenyan bean is brilliant. Harmony is the key to eudemonia, to la dolce vita, to ethical surefootedness; however, the ration isn't a continuum like the notes in a scale, which I've never learned, because my parents knew that my hands would be the tiny hands of a girl. At the end of the meal, I think in French. I want the waiter to say mademoiselle. I want to tug at his heart strings. I want his leather belt around my bean. I can balance on my hands.

Adaigo with Bell and Lantern

All my disobedient bodies cannot refuse
the allure of light bent by water or glass

as if I were a lanterned thing, more guest
then occupant: a small blaze of self at wick's end
as the iris in the field of the body is also the night's eye
fraught with half-shapes and phantoms
finding its way in the thinnest light

among the small and large catastrophes of fire --
the house, the car, the missing brother
the one who centered his life around the rung bell
gone among rivered and branching places
as will we or so say
those who know the weight of such matter:
all that can be measured in paper and ink
sent aloft by the unseasonal appetites of fire.

Gregory Mahrer

from The Small Republics of Other and Else

I received your first dispatch the summer I spent
petitioning the village headstones.

Where the fields folded in series of threes we were boundless.

We were not so good in doorways or public libraries.
Not great with spoons or swarms or remembering
to turn off streetlights as we passed.

The last draft of fall arrived, diagramming a year without winter.

Wearing our vanquished pelts we rehearse the early years.
What vexed us then vexes us still—our unbundled twenties,
narrow aperture of noon, urgencies built from false artifacts.

The indeterminate length of an hour.

Would we have been different had we lived in the villages
buried beneath ours? Could we have been the low garden,
audible flight, rivered sprawl?

*Body of silk, body rough with wool. How much you wanted
to unravel out of season.*

What will speak us once the storm of the body has passed.

Fever

My temperature clocked at 102 and kept rising.
I went to work anyway, manned a desk,
took room reservations, and oversaw meetings
until I left for home, delirious. Later, you called,
wanting to go out. I couldn't tell you I was sick.
I pulled my limp body to the car. At your house,
you were changing clothes. You bared your skin
but I felt ill. I could not go to a karaoke bar
or nightclub so I told you I needed to drive
with open windows. I took a dirt road
through a wooded area and landed
at a music festival where costumes were for sale,
some couture. I touched the cloth of what
I could not have: silk, cashmere, gabardine.
I sank into their softness and fell asleep
curled under racks of clothes, dreaming and sweating.

Your Door

I paused at your house: impatiens outside the front door,
a shock of color against the wood you painted dark green
to stand out in the neighborhood. I took the narrow cement path
lined with monkey grass that spilled over the walkway.
I stood at your door, noticed where the weather had chipped away
the paint, where you'd scraped and painted over. No screen door
to latch, no storm door to protect what you'd colored.
Then your voice, muted but clear: you asked someone to hold on.
You had to mention it more than once, as if the other person
wouldn't listen. I raised my hand, a closed fist with knuckles
pointed forward. If I announced myself here, at your front step,
you would tell me to wait, and it would be like always with you:
the days or months of silence, then your voice again.
And now your voice like a siren through door, asking
someone to hold on, someone who wouldn't let go.

Off-line

Where I would have wings,
you press
        your thumbs.
I look up, try to see
you shadowing behind me,

guess the angle
        of your jawbone.
You might have noticed my lips.
An easy red bulls-eye
had you aimed
        from that angle.

Or my toes.
        How I painted them
to match my lips, so you'd look
mouth to feet,
        up and down, once over.

Those thumbs,
        I want them pressed
into my obliques, not my shoulders.
Leave bruises like a badge,
        proof you were there.

Kiss Me

I want you to.
No, I don't.

I say it, but don't
mean it.

Damn the body, damn
the evening light.

It's all made
for love,

the spider,
and dew-laden web.

See the sun—
it slams against

our bare chests,
weeps

on our pleasure.
Kiss me here,

close your mouth
on my throat.

Kiss Me, Here

I want you to kiss me,
but not in front of your mother

or at the altar or beside
your old lover.

I want you to kiss me
with your tongue,

but not with
the other woman's

children peering from their
mattress on the floor.

I want you to kiss me
on my ear, from behind

while my hands are in
hot suds at the kitchen sink,

cinch your arms around
my hips, pin me,

but not while my fingers
seek the sharp knives.

I want you to kiss-kiss me
on the hollow of my arch,

feel your beard between
my toes, want my lips

to taste of blood,
wrists to bruise blue.

I want you to blow me
those breathy kisses that come.

What It Takes To Conceive

Heated kisses, rolling in wet fields,
hours of talking beneath moonlight,
a little wine, dirt, radishes,
brown eggs gathered from the morning lay,

rainy afternoons of *Moody Blues,*
fresh cut hay, geraniums' flashy blooms,
apple kuchen, coffee, and wood smoke.
The way steep narrow stairs hum

with weight of our feet, and outside
trees umbrella the paved road.
Voices come to us in night,
and we grasp their meaning.

There's an altar in the garden,
Mary Mother of God, but I'm not
Catholic, and can be so wrong.
Forgetfulness—the insignificant fact

of not being married when our daughter
was born. How others treated us with disdain,
and sent up prayers for the sin of us.
It took your thick black hair,

stocky thighs, the harmonica,
and the swinging of Grossmama's
good arm as we sang around her bed
in German I knew without study,
and my mustache as wetness of sea

clung to soft hairs under my nose,
and how you'd lean into me
to taste salt, our bodies sculpting
the warm sand. Sometimes I forget

what it took for us to make
our daughter, who grew
your long torso, and strong head.
Whose square face holds
beauty of the Rhine, and the tearing
down of Berlin's wall. She's a love
that forgives ours, that brings
things back to the light.

Natalie Giarratano

Surge

They say you can't take the thicket out of the girl, so bayou water swells under the uninterrupted Michigan snow. When winter plucks the last reeds from my head, I pretend it doesn't hurt (sends cotton-mouths crawling). This is the season for the danger in filling up too much—snakes have been known to crawl on roofs of flooded houses, fight for a spot to escape the dark humor of a hurricane. If you can cut through wood and shingle with muscle and axe—smoke-screens: the sun declares rights to flesh. Burning is imminent anyway, and it all burns—snake bites, snow, the melting away of a mouth.

RICHARD PRINS

It's My Birthday

and she's taken me like a silver wrapper in her mouth. The wine's quaffed and
sobs are riveting my sternum as she pumps me like a drowned sack of child. I
want to be childer, growner, anything but the years fuming out of my pores. We
broke up last week, and the week before. Now I'm dishes nameless in the sink.
I'm clothes wrinkling the floor. I'm the roaches cocking their slender antennae,
curious how our bodies crumble.

I wish it was tomorrow, so I go for a drink. The amber licks me inside. A mummy
jumps on his barstool, festooned in jewels. He is Billie Holiday and solitude flies
of his lips in rags. Tomorrow cracks my skull and makes me wish on the smaller
half, causing a banjo to stroll through the door, stepping on its train of chords.
The song unfurls where her legs are hooked on mine, squeezing. Let me make
this beautiful , she warns me. But my torso's still at the bar, pouring a truce spine-
deep that cleanses each bone passing through me.

TODD ROBINSON

Better to Lunch on TV than to Believe in Heaven

Breathing familiar myths, we belly up to the mountain.
Goddamn hyper-aware Sisyphus, Leonardo DiCaprio
makes you miserable. The universe a screaming beach
and the tide your life. You expected yes and yes, got
no and no. Are we volatile chemicals with memories?
Yes. And over time the next, then the next, then the next.

The White Pill
after Jim Carroll

I took the white pill this evening

I got new fuzz on the bones inside my skin

the missus
does her little sleep on the sofa

and at dawn
a whistle summons all the tiny workers
to their cubicles

it is silent and piercing

not at all like the shriek
of a perfectly failing republic

MATTHEW HUFF

What was left after you swallowed the whale and all the cosmos

You   said the coffee we shared was the color of bruised apples.
said my eyes were swollen, drowned apples.
said that every apple you ate reminded you of death, reminded you of Eve.
said you tried to push so many apologies through the ridges of my
      fingertips that I could choke on them.
said that when you did that, you could feel my heart.
said it felt rotten, past its prime, rotting fruit waiting for gnats to
      emerge from it.

You   said if I could find a tree filled with halos that I should cling to it.
said the angel's feet could untangle my hair.
said maybe they'd cut Absalom free as well.

I   had a lungful of cotton and no tongue.
had kept eyes in a snowglobe—green marbles cracking against the pane.
had something so heavy and so dense inside that I severed the space
      between my hand and yours.

I   had nothing to say so I swallowed the needle and thread.

You   said that the night had never seemed brighter than that first night we
      spent together balanced between the barrier dividing the freeway.
said that memories made things more tangible.
said that the stars had such density because they were made of
      something penetrable, invisible.
said that the closer we look at something, the more it disappears.
said if I was in the center of the star there would be nothing to see but the
      tornado of energy.
said that we, as humans, shared the same basic energy and composition
      that the stars did.

You   said that we could burn so much brighter and longer if we didn't let the
      density of our hearts suck us into ourselves.
said not to become a Red Giant, a Black Hole.

You   said you believed the stars, from space, could see us burning.

from The Alter Ego Handbook

My alter ego uses Photoshop to conceal his flaws, posts photos on the internet that approximate perfection. My alter ego has a Facebook page and Twitter account, though I'm not into social media. He claims there's too much identity in anonymity, too much authenticity. I tell him image isn't everything, but he continues blogging excerpts from his unfinished manifesto and obsessing about reputation. There are too many variables in obscurity; it's as futile as seeking privacy in a world full of windows. My alter ego incessantly tinkers with his smartphone, recites factoids during conversations to appear witty. He's a con artist imitating a renaissance man. He has every scenario scripted, knows when to gaze at the audience and recite the perfect line, exit stage left.

ADRIAN POTTER

from The Alter Ego Handbook

My alter ego always says humiliation like that, slowly and with emphasis on
the wrong syllable. He's a bonafide showoff, a made-for-TV attention whore of
the illest repute. Always overdressing and overspending while I blend into the
background. All about flash, panache, the blatant art of making a splash. He
claims to be so overt that it's covert, that standing out makes him outstanding. By
now all my secrets are public domain. My insecurities are tethered to my exterior
like enormous shiny sequins. I fear leaving mostly because I fear I will never
return. I fear returning because it feels like leaving over and over again. My alter
ego loves revision. The dubbed-over mixtape, the edited bible verse, the subtle
mutations of identity. My alter ego always says humiliation like it's a threat.

What Would Captain Do?

Lost in another barroom afternoon,
Captain watches over the place with his good eye;
it's has seen such terrible things.
Says he don't trust no-one but The Metronome,
who's sat in the corner gnawing on mutton chops
and slurping up sea suds. Captain's advices are balanced
upon medieval moral constructs.
Fuck 'em all, he says,
and at six-foot six, he easily fishes up anyone
by the lapels, including today's big-talking young'un.
You scared, boy? You haunted?
Someone hacked yer tongue?
Sunbeams spear through the window
and play on Captain's beard,
showing off the fire between his words.
Amplify yer quiet sadness, boy.
Captain's counsel lands like a dull thud
to the heavy bag, his voice as rough
as concrete chips poured from a beer stein.
Come back when you've got more
about you than a few almost tales, boy.
He points to the parking lot
with his index stump,
the extra lost to the teeth
of a bandsaw. His breath tastes like linseed oil.
The kid sneezes like a shot-up tin can, before
walking back into the day. Captain waves
like the boy is leaving on a ship.
The trick, Captain calls, is to act
like you'll blow yer top any minute.
The Metronome sighs;
he's heard this all before.

*

Here comes The Metronome
trudging up the back stairs.
He's back early.
Captain will still be winning and losing
friends, throwing back schooners

of Fish House Punch and White Russians
until his voice booms
like a nor'wester-caught spinnaker, until
someone's fist says, enough is enough.
He'll be carried back to his bunk, though –
hard to like, easy to love - jawbone broke,
but whistling a jaunty shanty.
The Metronome, faking sleep,
unconscious, incognito, a scuttled sailor
waiting for what the world owes him.
His head is full of unwritten words
and an unremitting string of tuts,
tut-tut-tut.

The Instinctual Turbulence Of The Man Beneath The Man

I dreamt I was dreaming in the arms of a disappearing
day, and when I woke I couldn't make head nor tails
of the online analysis site. We were driving
on the Pamplona ring-road, The Metronome
gunning it too fast and saying something in Swiss-German
about dog tears being an ointment for an inflamed temper.
The morning was as soft as inner thigh flesh chafed
into tenderness and I was surely a barely functioning alcoholic –
Captain had stopped pretending otherwise years before.
The heavenly pattern of traffic cones contained all
the encrypted secrets of creation, like the oak leaf's
brutal symmetry, a doctrine of unflinching sacrifice
for anyone who doesn't follow the path into the contraflow.
We were delivering a shopping bag full of human ears
that The Metronome had won in a game of three-card brag
and promptly lost in a high Chicago, low Chicago double-up attempt.
I woke again into a sun-slowed morning, like something dissolving
in my hands underneath a blinking porch light. I was dating a girl
called Wendy who I'd met at In-N-Out Burger. It's like how my third
favourite number happens to be three, after seven and nine - spooky.
I knew Wendy knew Captain
and The Metronome, but I didn't want to know how well.
I woke again. Captain was talking up big over a breakfast of orange soda
and cigarettes. He does exactly what he wants, which is normally absolutely
nothing. Personality is just the ability to appreciate ambiguity,
he said, like a child who wins your attention by threatening violence
towards you, or themself.

TIM CRAVEN

Happy Hour

On the six inch-high stage, a local post-modern skiffle band
is thrashing out badly-done covers of despair, the singer mewling
her lyrics from scribblings on the back of a bank statement.
The barman looks around for a glass to refill, his smile askew
like a badly-buttoned cardigan. This palace of false-hearted solutions,
necrotic like the steel-ribbed skeleton of a bankrupt office block.

This is where loneliness ends, crumbling in your hands. In the corner,
on stools they claim as their own, Captain and The Metronome,
the two great outliers.

The Metronome, acting the fop in his five-buck Salvy sports jacket,
free-falling to such deliberate depths that the only course
of manoeuvre was to cut him off completely, which broke
his mother's heart. Social mobility hitting reverse.
But he's never been on a roof in the dead of night
sliding saddleback ridge-tiles off the eaves of a blacking factory
because a punter was willing to pay top whack for authenticity.

Captain, conversely, clawed his way out of the gradual advance
of oxidation, from a place where everything you touch puts grease marks
on your shirt. But he's never been so lost in the swamped rhythm
of scotch as to put his last hundred on a 66-1 reverse forecast
and failed to focus across the track to see his horse pulling up short.

Evolving from scamps to tinkers to tearaways to rascals
to ruffians to cold blooded opportunists. They share a love of the pool table's
slate-bed flatness, running their fingertips over the threadbare felt. Drinking hard
and dumbing down to bypass all the slow signs of mortality.

These are not feelings, but memories of things they once felt.
You scratch the surface, you get more surface. As American as the dream
of a televised marriage proposal; that big daytime moment amongst
the missing teeth and pregnant foul-mouthed daughters.
Making beauty, throwing it away, making more.

Captain and The Metronome argue over who is the ball and who is the chain;
they can't accept that they can't be separated.
The Metronome has gone a little misty. This feeling is too enormous.

Captain Finds Work

Since he walked from the midnight shift
at the meat packing plant, after another light
wage packet, Captain looks like he's one more
rough night away from collecting cans on garbage day.
The Metronome has ponied up this week's rent
from his assistant bookie job at the track.

Captain says he's found work running with a new crew
stripping wire and copper pipe from the singed
drywall of burnouts - insurance jobs so the owners
can leave town. He unravels then coils-up the nest of tangles,
cuts the plumbing into three-foot lengths, and hauls himself
onto the roof to pilfer the lead valleys like wrenching out
dead men's gold teeth. When the houses are slow
he goes to the train tracks like some stop-motion colossus
tippy-toeing over the electrified rails, in a boiled wool coat,
black against a periwinkle sky, as desperate and off kilter
as a Mumbai lean-to. He makes off with all the copper-rope
he can carry, which is why the trains are down today
and The Metronome is late for work, stuck in a carriage
going nowhere.

Eat Something

The food has grown not moldy
but barbed. To eat is to fish
if my tongue were a worm. I can't shield

myself from the fact of geese dying
of fish line and hook obstruction.
Every crumb is a bezoar. I spun

a spoon a million rotations
over the stove, fattened
my husband, patted his rotunda,
delivered too many beers to count. Now

I dole sharp grapes down my gullet.
Food gives you energy.
I peck a crusty bread because
food is life is a thing
they say when they tell me to eat.

The life travels
through goose esophagus,
through body sleeve.
It does reward energy

to resist the want
to quell the rumbling
of my husband's stomach
where he thins across town.

CINDY HUNTER MORGAN

Deckhand: Scent Theory

When he climbed up the deck ladder
that first morning, his shirt still smelled
of his mother's wash line:
Dreft and sunshine.

Now what he breathes is rain
and ore, deck paint, grease,
engine oil, boiler exhaust,
steam.

Mornings there is coffee.
Sometimes he pours a bit
on the cuff of his sleeve
so later he can press his nose in it.

Still, what blows in from the deck
is metallic and sharp-edged:
wind scraped by steel
mixed with hydraulic fluid.

It is not enough to air
the passageways, which reek of sweat:
glandular and primal,
a condensation of what is repressed.

His own body is slick with it.
At night he peels
his clothes off
and drops them in a pile,

dark, stagnant puddle
of stained cotton,
cesspool of sweat turning
to mildew.

CINDY HUNTER MORGAN

Deckhand: Dream Theory

He falls into sleep
headlong, as though into water.
Every night a sudden descent,
his body spread, weightless,

striped pajamas
ballooning near ankles.
His feet: white,
pale as bone under moonlight.

Some nights he flips on his back,
flutter kicks the sheets,
drifts until his brain waves
slow, his heart settles.

Whatever comes to him
in that stretch of deep
sleep—a sturgeon bigger
than the ship, a storm –

whatever comes,
he keeps breathing,
the rise and fall of his chest
as rhythmic as the boat.

Deckhand: Color Theory

He was green, just out of school,
and still had a boy's expectations
of color. Days on a ship, he assumed,
would be cyan and yellow—

blue water, a gold circle
fixed in a clear sky. A few afternoons
came close. More often,
the lake was the color of slate;

the sun, pale and weak.
Piss, they called it. No women
to scold the deckhands.
Mornings when the water was gray,

it looked hard, something
that could split your head open.
Real color was elsewhere:
red of rusting steel,

red of his own blood
rising in thin beads
when he sliced his finger
on a hatch cover.

Orange ring buoys. White life boats,
a kind of hope. Not enough.
Deep black of starless nights
and unventilated cargo holds

packed with coal and methane
and the threat of combustion.
Combustion: more red,
more orange, and something

close to yellow, but not the yellow
he imagined. All of it flashing
in sparks that sank in water
too deep for language.

Zzz

If sleep teased us, we inhaled
busy-pills. If it hazed us, we swallowed
mosquitoes and held our tongues
to the zapper. If it counted us
sheep, our count went from three bays
of neighbor hounds to eight stray
gunshots to how many nanoseconds
before sunrise. Who knew how many
tweakers it took to unscrew
a fluorescent bulb? The first answer
was *bzzzt*, but *zero* was better
lest we cause the darkness.
The best answer was not to answer.
Sleep called us deadbeats. It called us
after midnight and threatened
to repossess our hours,
or made no sound except to breathe
blackout curtains in our ears.
Nobody called the police
fuzz because it felt like down pillows
pressed down atop our airways.
Though the sirens weren't *that* type,
those cops and their noise
of choppers and coffee machines
tempted us more than the daydream
we never told anybody,
so whoever guessed it must have spied.
Some dreamers fought to get in bed
with sleep. To get inside
their heads, we needed to fix
both eyelids wide and show flashcards
for *bullhorn* and *bulldozer*. No doze
could go on when we shook the babies
awake with jackhammer earthquakes.
Alarm-clock buttons said *snooze*
and *chainsaws*, but if we hit either,
the readout froze on *forget it.*

STEVEN D. SCHROEDER

The Road

Best turn back. Just trouble ahead.
But we'd seen behind. With one hand
on an automatic pistol's grip,
our wheelmen used fear to steer
past barricades propped up by law
and plywood, past state-trooper types
whose mirrorshades reflected the object
might be closer than it appeared,
past spike strips that didn't exist
according to the last printed map.
The mountains could provide a hideout.
Forget guides, fuck survival—
city kids needed skyscrapers
toppled across eight lanes of blacktop.
Besides, we heard enough bad news
was oozing from the mineshafts.
We played chicken with the broken
brakelights of abandoned tanker trucks,
that in adrenaline's red revelation
we might believe the voice of Jesus
on *in case of rapture* bumper stickers
and emergency broadcast loops.
Exit your vehicle. Do not attempt escape.
The whirlwind gained ground so fast
its gusts navigated our beater Neons
clear through the ruin we knew
once the GPS quit its misleadership.
A vagrant and his *the end
is near* cardboard sign, both lying
half in a ditch, doomsaid some more
before the fever wasted him away.
*If you get to where you fall,
you've gone too far.* Wider than eyes
that luminesced along the offramps
and we prayed belonged to wolves,
the horizon promised we could reach
whatever lied on its sun-touched side.
We traveled to *inevitable*, driven
home by the nailgun *thump-thump*

speech of speedbumps, potholes,
bodies: *wrong way, wrong way, so long.*

STEVEN D. SCHROEDER

Literally

Bad words weren't the only words
to be bad. From television, we heard
uh huh huh, uh huh huh huh.
Our vocabulary was the biggest
collective dick-joke in the universe.
We stockpiled dictionaries
to prevent their consumption—
which meant not *reading*
but *burning* and *eating*—
because we believed their heaviness
pluperfect to quash passive voices.
As if we lived in Soviet Russia,
syntax tortured us. Like society,
crumbled sentence structure.
Compound slummed to join
any sketchy noun from *bow*
and *fracture* to *chemical* and *cult.*
Lose got loose, and we almost lost
our scold fingers style-guiding it
back to its pen. The pen itself
scrawled *sic* again and again
until it sickened us enough
to sic English mastiffs on it.
Rules written in disappearing ink
couldn't order military intervention,
much less an alphabet, so the police
set up metal detectors and a profile
for every unattended letter.
Predicates became subject
to traffic stops and spellchecks,
and they never did what we said
or said what we did. Even numbers
went from informants to dissenters
to hunted. If prepositions wanted
to end our lines, we shot at and into
through. Caught in crossfire, *literally*
doublecrossed. We wouldn't lie
or lay about it. We executed all verbs

except one. The only good language
we ever saw was dead.

Charles Harper Webb

You Don't Know Beans

When Mom heard me yell, "Aw fudge,"
she pictured square-cut chocolate bricks
heaped, sweet and sticky, on a china
plate—not sweaty nudes grunting
and grappling in the throes of making life.

When she said, "Poo," she saw a cute bear;
"Shoot," a curly-headed cupid tugging
at love's golden bow—never the slag
from life's foundry, dropped on the sidewalk
where the homeless cadge spare change.

When she said "Gee," or in extremis,
added "Whiz," she saw the letter's
barbed fish-hook; she saw orange
cheese-food, not a crucified peacenik
who shrieked God's hallowed name in vain.

Heck was a cough, not a pit spewing
sulfur and black flame. Wee-wee
was tiny. Pee-pee was a little bird.
Dick was President; pecker, a red-crowned
hammer-head. Darn was for socks;

dang was cousin to ding-dong bell.
Pussy was a poor, drenched kitty in a well.
When I told my sister, "Aw, you don't
know beans," Mom thought of limas,
string, pinto, kidney (indelicate name,

but good for you), and vowed to teach Sis
how to cook, and gave no thought
to airy by-products of legume-digestion—
from whence, with what unholy sounds,
they came.

Raising Hell

In film after film, The Wicked summon
Satan—knifing babies on stone altars;
rutting with black-hooded fiends, chanting

blasphemies carved into human skin.
Each time, Big S almost slips in. The sky chars
black, as lightning carves it into chunks.

The earth quakes. Thunder shakes
a crumbling castle's walls. Its roof blasts open
to reveal a giant lizard, or a maw in the sky

from which a blinding light flames down.
And yet, things never go quite right.
Baal's priest falls, the spell's last syllable dead

on his tongue. Red-eyed Baby Beelzebub
blows up. Scalded by holy text, the Great Lizard
yoyos back into its black cave in the sky

while organizers of the cosmic coup,
who hoped to rule the world forever,
or at least become rap stars, are crushed

by scaly claws; snatched, howling, into hell;
flattened by falling rocks; or vaporized—
inverted crosses, bloody robes, and all.

Satan never gets to see demons rule
Congress; ghouls in every courtroom;
high-rises putrescent with zombies; freeways

paved with boiling pitch, jammed
with drivers who shriek, and slam their horns,
and flash their hot-coal eyes.

Elegy

Myrna Loy's been stolen from her prime
years ago. You saw it in her ankles,
thick as pines, that nose—stripped by time

of their elegance and sweep. It's a crime
no punishment could stop, this troubling
of our star, spun off from her prime.

Must human beauty dwindle to a rind
tattooed with liver spots, scored with wrinkles?
Those ankles, those rheumy eyes. No charm

could save that face and figure, so sublime
they made the wily Dillinger less careful,
dreaming of her partnership in crime.

She played the perfect wife, the critics chimed
in chorus till they saw wattles dangling
beneath that smile, breath-stopping in its time.

Yet most of us grow old. We shouldn't pine
over one loss in a blight so universal.
But Myrna Loy's been stolen from her prime,
her cosy glamor grub for the glutton time.

WILLIAM TROWBRIDGE

Hier Gibt es Blaubeeren
(Here there are blueberries)

> *Caption on photos of SS women auxiliaries being served blueberries on a July 22, 1944, day-trip to Solahutte, recreation center for staff at Auschwitz-Birkenau, 18 miles away.*

The women perch, like birds, along a deck rail:
"Mmmm, good," they mime, giggling as they
ham it up behind big spoonfuls, some with mouths
agape, nestling style, while a demure civilian
accordionist pumps out Nordic forest hymns.

But it's not all fun in this photo-story, which turns
like a children's homily. In the last shot, the berries
are all eaten, shown by the women, who hold out
empty bowls. Some look wistful, others mock tears,
all having been such greedy little birds.

ANGELINA OBERDAN

The Dead Roadside Doe

Today the dead doe's guts spill like a pomegranate
split open across the roadside's platter. The corpse
has been there for two days, pivoting slightly,
each time truck tires stir its rest. I noticed it
appear just after we broke up, but I'm not sure
what happened to its legs; it has always seemed
legless, all body, as though the limbs were the first
to be grabbed by vultures and drug into the trees.
And the doe's head, I never saw its head or skull;
maybe it was buck, not a doe at all, not an innocent,
and its skull was sawed off by whoever hit it
to be mounted like the antlers from a prize shot are
in someone's wood-paneled den. But I don't think
that's right; I think it was a doe wandering across
the road in the evening to seek sweeter clover, without
enough reason for wanting it, just wanting something else.

Caseus

"How can anyone be expected to govern a country with 325 cheeses?"
—*Charles de Gaulle*

Caesar ate his first blue cheese
just west of Rocquefort,
in the town of Saint-Affrique.
In Latin it was *caseus,*
which became *cacio* in Italian,
queso in Spanish, *quejio*
in Portuguese. Cheese.
The Roman farmer Columella
described how to get rennet
from the fourth stomach
of a lamb, how to add it
to fresh milk, how long to wait
for the milk to curdle,
how to press the whey out,
how to salt the curds until dry.
In *The Odyssey*, the Cyclops
drained his curds in wicker baskets
lining the walls of his cave.
The baskets gave the cheese
its form—in Greek *formos*—
in Italian *formaggio*, in French
fromage. Virgil ate fresh cheese
with chestnuts. The techniques
of ripening and airing, *affinage,*
are secrets passed down
thousands of years. Right now,
in some cave in France,
a farmer is carefully turning
each wheel, salting one side,
watching the mold emerge.

SIMON PERCHIK

*

You were so sure! the boxes
sealed and no one
getting a bead on you

—wherever you're moving
it would be by air–not the kind
that comes from runways

but cardboard, corrugated
where its turbulence is hidden
at least till high enough

safely under your arms
still closing the flaps
and though the wings are taped

they're already breaking apart
held the heading too long
—you thought this place

would last out the month
not burn to the floor
become winds and your emptiness.

Simon Perchik

*

There is no tunnel, you crawl
the way a turtle takes hold
and from the sidewalk a dry breeze

smelling from salt and two in the afternoon
—the crowd thinks the cup is for beggars
fill it so the air inside

will rise and you can breathe
one more time: a tide
lets you survive in the open

though one cheek is dragged
over the other till your mouth
becomes a shell—all you can do

is drink from it
do what skies once did
filled with thirst and emptiness.

Simon Perchik

*

Without any flowers
you are still breathing
—without a throat

still eating the warm air
though what's left from the sun
is no longer blue

hides the way your grave
is covered with stones
and still hungry

—you could use more stones
a heaviness to become your arms
one for working harder

the other invisible
leaving your heart
lifts from the dirt

your mouth, your eyes
and the sky letting go the Earth
as if you weigh too much.

Simon Perchik

*

As if it finished its last meal this log
sits back, waits inside for the stove
the way ashes roll over and all around you

trees are burning on rivers
that came from the first fire
still settling down as thirst

and the heady smoke flames leave behind
to be remembered by—from day one
their slow climbing turns, at first

threatening to gut the place and now
you can't live without them though your fingers
after so many years have become airborne

safe from the dangerous shadows all night
dripping between each breath and your mouth
left open—you pour in wood

to get death started :an arriving flame
surrounded by the Earth and tiny holes
—it's the only way you know how.

SIMON PERCHIK

*

Just a toy though the string
is still afraid, tied as if inside
a weightlessness is pulling it
closer and closer and can't let go
caged in on all sides
by the color blue and emptiness

—a trapped balloon, banded
the way all buoys spread out
and the channel lurking below
unravels as rain that has no water yet

—it's always been like this
at carnivals, balloons by the hundreds
coming from a single fountain
that never falls back

—you can't take in enough air
—your arms leak and you drown
in the overcast that has no shadow yet
not yet touching down in the cry
from your hands over your heart.

ADAM LOVE

Red Pining for the Summer Lover

Who heard the porch banjo
while you walked him through
the gravel-studded streets and fled
into that dark house above the headstones.

Who felt the city lightscape gutting
that black room you took him in to rest.

I have painted your story in every maple leaf
that will turn red. I have kept your street nickels
in the ashtray. I have swallowed your mosquitos
in my sleep. And still, you rain.

But for the flood, might the stars wet my dreams.
But for the flavor of venison, might the hunters weep.

The kale-green scent of Russian Olive
blossoms drifts in through the shades.

And I feel you, like the purple-orange sunset
in the heat of car exhaust: burning loudly
enough for any forgotten god.

ADAM LOVE

If I could say the cosmonaut is not my father

1.

then I wouldn't have to tell you
that he shouldn't have married the woman
who bore me—I wouldn't have to explain
how he killed himself in a November snowstorm,
missing a curve in his angry Saab.

I wouldn't have to remind myself
of all that childhood
let me forget: that Starbursts
are nature's manufactured way of reminding
the living what sunlight particles taste like.

I wouldn't have to create subterranean chambers
without doors to represent his undying anguish
of falling in and out of love.

I could just state things. Accurate things.

I could say that clouds are water, suspended
in a gaseous state, and hold no other meaning,
aside from being the animated caricature
of human imagination.

I could say that magpies
are annoying thieves, and that once,
at seventeen, my best friend threw a golf ball
at one and hit it right upside the head,
killing it instantly. And that after poking
its exposed and swollen brain tissue with a sharp stick
found in the tall grass, we tossed its corpse somewhere
deep within the field,
and laughed away our guilt for hours.

2.

I'm not really in the mood
to tell you more stories,

Adam Love

not sure if secrets are revealed
to a midnight dreamer—
whether I sleep or write.

It's just that sometimes I read Rilke
and weep as if I were rain in an oak leaf.
But then I'll move into some sonnet
and have no idea what the fuck
is going on.

Is life really that serious?

I mean, if I could take a bouquet
of yellow roses and throw
them from a cliff, would I be
living a poem?

      Would you be watching?

I guess
it's only a matter
of perspective.

People have been doing it for years.

      Basho in his old pond,
      Yeats and his nursery rhymes.

But, I mean, could I really
say anything for a gravedigger
who works in a tractor?

Or for the archer
whose bow has broken,
what poem could I write for him?

      Once I catapulted
      Myself across three
      Fields.

Adam Love

I landed in a patch of ferns,
Didn't get one scratch…

Maybe, I could say that tonight, it's more
than metaphor seeping through my veins.

Or that maybe it's less.

Maybe I could just finally say
that I'm only looking for a wind
to rattle my bones.

CONTRIBUTORS

Julie Brooks Barbour is the author of *Small Chimes* (Aldrich Press, 2014) and two chapbooks: *Earth Lust* (Finishing Line Press, 2014) and *Come To Me and Drink* (Finishing Line Press, 2012). Her poems have appeared in *Waccamaw, diode, storySouth, Prime Number Magazine, The Rumpus, Midwestern Gothic, Blue Lyra Review,* and *Verse Daily.* She is co-editor of the journal *Border Crossing* and an Associate Poetry Editor at *Connotation Press: An Online Artifact.* She teaches composition and creative writing at Lake Superior State University.

Jackson Burgess studies at the University of Southern California, where he is a Mark Greenberg Fellow for Poetry and Editor in Chief of *Fractal Literary Magazine.* Jackson has placed work in *Rattle, Word Riot, Bartleby Snopes, Tin House Flash Fridays,* and elsewhere, and lives at jacksonburgess.com.

Adriana Cloud's work has appeared in *The Rumpus, Armchair/Shotgun, The Nervous Breakdown,* the *New Orleans Review,* and others. She lives in Boston, where she works in book publishing and argues about commas a lot. She's read Harry Potter in three languages. You can find her on Twitter at @adicloud.

Rebecca Connors was raised in the suburbs of Washington, D.C. and received her BA in English from Boston University. After trying multiple cities, she is back in Boston where she writes poetry and works as a digital strategist. Find her on Twitter at @aprilist

Thomas Cook lives in Massachusetts, where he edits *Tammy.*

Originally from Stoke-on-Trent, England, **Tim Craven** was a neuroscientist living in London until he began a poetry MFA at Syracuse University. In 2014, his poems have appeared in *The Lascaux Review, New Delta Review, Fjords Review, Sonora Review, CURA, Eleven Eleven, Switchback, New Madrid, Natural Bridge* and others. He sometimes tweets: @CravenTim

Sage Curtis is an MFA candidate at University of San Francisco. As a writer, she is preoccupied with the grime of cities, everything from the back alleys to the rooftops. Her work has been published other literary journals such as *Garbanzo Literary Journal, Perceptions Magazine, Deep Waters* and *34th Parallel,* amongst others. She is the assistant fiction editor at *The Rumpus* and a jack-of-all-trades at PushPen Press. She also received the Dorrit Sibley Award for Poetry from San Jose State University.

CONTRIBUTORS

Nandini Dhar is the author of the chapbook *Lullabies Are Barbed Wire Nations* (Two of Cups Press, 2014). Her poems have recently appeared or are forthcoming in *Potomac Review, PANK, Los Angeles Review, Whiskey Island, Cream City Review* and elsewhere. She is the co-editor of the journal *Elsewhere*. Nandini hails from Kolkata, India, and divides her time between her hometown and Miami, Florida, where she works as an Assistant Professor of English at Florida International University.

Katherine Frain is one of those annoying people who refuses to drink coffee. This life choice, she tells herself, is balanced out by the decision to edit poetry for the *Blueshift Journal*, which has been incredibly rewarding thus far. Frain's work has been recognized by the National YoungArts Foundation and the Poetry Society of London, and her work is also forthcoming or published in *The Journal, Sugared Water,* and *Vector Press,* among others. She currently resides in New Jersey, where she's experiencing her first real Northern winter.

Natalie Giarratano's first collection of poems, *Leaving Clean,* won the 2013 Liam Rector First Book Prize in Poetry (Briery Creek Press, 2013). Recent poems appear or are forthcoming in *Gulf Stream: Poems of the Gulf Coast, Isthmus Review, Tupelo Quarterly, Laurel Review, Best New Poets,* and *TYPO,* among others. She co-edits *Pilot Light,* an online journal of 21st century poetics and criticism, teaches writing at American University, and lives in Northern Virginia with her partner and their pup.

Charles Harper Webb's latest book, *What Things Are Made Of* was published by the University of Pittsburgh Press in 2013. Recipient of grants from the Whiting and Guggenheim foundations, Webb teaches Creative Writing at California State University, Long Beach.

Lydia Havens lives and writes near Tucson, Arizona. She is the Executive Poetry Editor for *Transcendence Magazine* and an intern for Spoken Futures, Inc. Her work has previously been published or is forthcoming in *Vademecum Magazine, FreezeRay Poetry, Blue Monday Review,* and *Words Dance,* among other places. Lydia is a slam poet who has been featured at events such as Tucson Poetry Festival and Words on the Avenue. In April 2014, she placed second at the Tucson Youth Poetry Slam's All City Championships.

Contributors

Matthew Huff is the Assistant-Editor at *Poemoftheweek.org* and is a first-grade teacher at a school named after a Mexican anarchist. Matthew studied Creative Writing at the University of Colorado Denver where he was an associate editor for the journal *Copper Nickel*; Matthew also holds a degree in Elementary Education from Colorado Christian University. His work has recently appeared or is forthcoming in *Chicago Quarterly Review, Meat for Tea: The Valley Review, Jelly Bucket, The Allegheny Review, Word Riot,* and *Paragon.* Matthew lives near Denver with his wife, two dogs, and a kitty he is allergic to.

Cindy Hunter Morgan teaches creative writing at Michigan State University and is the author of two chapbooks. *The Sultan, The Skater, The Bicycle Maker* won The Ledge Press 2011 Poetry Chapbook Competition; *Apple Season* won the Midwest Writing Center's 2012 Chapbook Contest, judged by Shane McCrae. Her poems have appeared in a variety of journals, including *West Branch, Bateau,* and *Sugar House Review.* Poems from her new manuscript about Great Lakes shipwrecks appear or are forthcoming in several journals, including *Midwestern Gothic, Fogged Clarity,* and *Salamander.*

Lillian Kwok lives and studies in Sweden. Her work appears or is forthcoming in *Hawaii Pacific Review, Salt Hill, NANO Fiction* and other journals. She holds an MFA in writing from Vermont College of Fine Arts.

Diane Lockward is the author of *The Crafty Poet: A Portable Workshop* (Wind Publications, 2013) and three poetry books, most recently *Temptation by Water.* Her previous books are *What Feeds Us,* which received the 2006 Quentin R. Howard Poetry Prize, and *Eve's Red Dress,* all from Wind Publications. Her poems have been included in such journals as *Harvard Review, Spoon River Poetry Review,* and *Prairie Schooner.* Her work has also been featured on *Poetry Daily, Verse Daily, Gwarlingo,* and *The Writer's Almanac.*

Adam Love's work appears in (or is upcoming in) *Split Lip Magazine, Black Tongue Review, Ampersand Review, Revolver, Sugar House Review, Atticus Review, Metazen, Main Street Rag,* among others. He's the author of the the chapbook, *Another Small Fire* (Tired Hearts Press 2013). He runs the Literary Arts portion of the Utah Arts Festival. In his free time, he's in between surfing the Pacific Ocean or exploring the mountains and western rivers of Utah

Contributors

Greg Mahrer's work has been published in *The New England Review, The Indiana Review, Green Mountains Review, Volt, Colorado Review, Haden's Ferry Review* and elsewhere as well as the web sites *Poetry Daily* and *Verse Daily*. Several of his poems have been nominated for Pushcart Prizes. His current manuscript, *A Provisional Map of the Lost Continent*, has been a finalist for the Sawtooth Prize from Ahsahta Press as well as the first book prize from Four Way Books and the T.S. Elliot prize from Truman State University.

Bill Neumire's first book, *Estrus*, was a semi-finalist for the 42 Miles Press Award, and recent work appears in *Berkeley Poetry Review, Linebreak, Barrow Street,* and *Laurel Review*. In addition, he currently serves as an assistant editor for *Verdad*.

Angelina Oberdan earned her MFA in Creative Writing (Poetry) at McNeese State University in Lake Charles, Louisiana, and is currently an instructor at Central Piedmont Community College. Most days she sits at her kitchen table and stares out of the window at her yard, and on rare days, she actually writes something. Her poems are forthcoming or have been published in various journals including *Yemassee, Cold Mountain Review, Italian Americana, Louisiana Literature*, and *Southern Indiana Review.*

Simon Perchik is an attorney whose poems have appeared in *Partisan Review, The Nation, Poetry, The New Yorker,* and elsewhere. His most recent collection is *Almost Rain*, published by River Otter Press (2013). For more information, including free e-books, his essay titled "Magic, Illusion and Other Realities" please visit his website at www.simonperchik.com

Amy Plettner is a Nebraska writer, living and working on the prairie in the southeastern part of the state. Her poetry has appeared in a variety of anthologies and journals, most recently, Rattle, Prairie Wind, and The Untidy Season. Her first book of poetry, Undoing Orion's Belt, is the 7th of the Kloefkorn series from WSC Press, 2011. She holds an MFA in writing from University of Nebraska.

Adrian Potter writes both poetry and fiction and is the author of the short fiction chapbook *Survival Notes* (Červená Barva Press, 2008). He won first prize in the 2010 Southern Illinois Writers Guild Poetry Contest and the 2006 Červená Barva Press Fiction Chapbook Prize, among other awards. Some recent publication credits include *The Broken Plate, Tidal Basin Review* and *Mythium*. Additional propaganda can be found at http://adrianspotter.squarespace.com/

Richard Prins is a New Yorker who sometimes lives in Dar es Salaam. He received his MFA degree from New York University. He is currently a poetry mentor with Hunts Point Alliance For Children, and poetry editor for the new literary series Ink.ed MFA. His poems appear in places like *Baltimore Review, Barrow Street, Cimarron Review, Los Angeles Review, Painted Bride Quarterly, Rattle, Redivider,* and *Thrush Poetry Journal.*

Kim Roberts is the author of four books of poems, most recently *To The South Pole,* a series of connected blank verse sonnets in the voice of Antarctic explorer Robert Falcon Scott (Broadkill Press, 2015). She is the editor of the journal *Beltway Poetry Quarterly,* the anthology *Full Moon on K Street: Poems About Washington, DC* (Plan B Press, 2010), and the web exhibit DC Writers' Homes.

Todd Robinson's words have appeared in *Sugar House Review, Margie, Prairie Schooner, The Southeast Review, Midwest Quarterly, Natural Bridge, The Potomac Review, M/C: A Journal of Media and Culture,* and many other venues.

Steven D. Schroeder's second book, *The Royal Nonesuch* (Spark Wheel Press 2013). His poetry is available or forthcoming in *Barrow Street, Crab Orchard Review,* and *Cream City Review.* He edits the online journal *Anti-,* co-curates the Observable Reading Series, and works as a Certified Professional Resume Writer.

Leah Sewell is assistant editor at Coconut Poetry, an MFA graduate of the University of Nebraska, and a book designer, poet, and mother. Her work has appeared or is forthcoming in *[PANK], Midwestern Gothic, Weave Magazine* and *Spry.* Her chapbook, *Birth in Storm,* was the winner of the 2012 ELJ Publications Chapbook Competition.

Molly Sutton Kiefer is the author of the hybrid essay *Nestuary* (Ricochet Editions, 2014) and the poetry chapbooks *The Recent History of Middle Sand Lake* (Astounding Beauty Ruffian Press, 2010) and *City of Bears* (dancing girl press, 2013). Her work has appeared in *The Collagist, Harpur Palate, Women's Studies Quarterly, WomenArts Quarterly, Berkeley Poetry Review,* and *Southampton Review,* among others. She is a founding editor of *Tinderbox*

Contributors

Poetry Journal, reviews for *PANK* and *The Rumpus*, and runs Balancing the Tide: Motherhood and the Arts | An Interview Project. More can be found at www.mollysuttionkiefer.com.

William Trowbridge's latest poetry collection is *Put This On, Please: New and Selected Poems* (Red Hen Press 2014). His other collections are *Ship of Fool, The Complete Book of Kong, Flickers, O Paradise,* and *Enter Dark Stranger*. He lives in the Kansas City area and teaches in the University of Nebraska Low-residency MFA in Writing Program. He is Poet Laureate of Missouri.

Spark Wheel Press
www.sparkwheelpress.com

Now Accepting Submissions

The Royal Nonesuch

Steven D. Schroeder

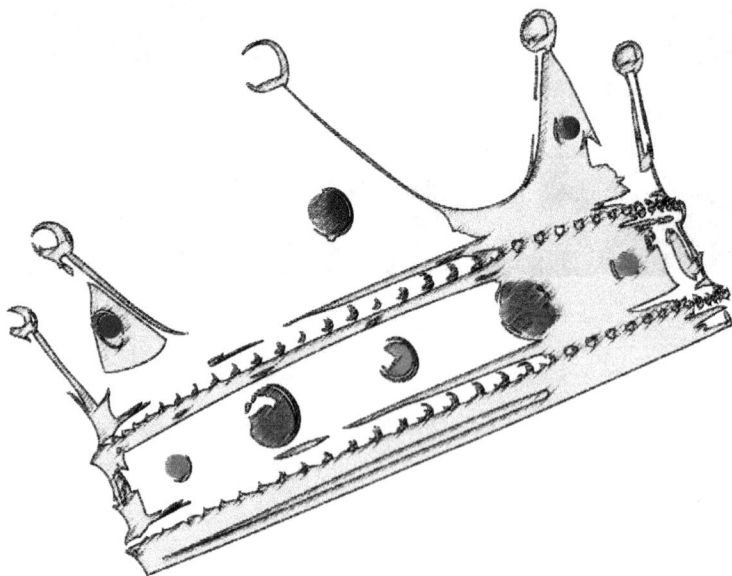

SparkWheelPress

THE UNPAINTED SHORE

C Dylan Bassett

SparkWheelPress

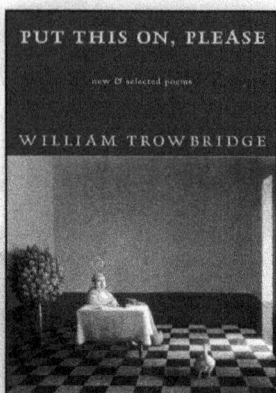

PUT THIS ON, PLEASE

new & selected poems

WILLIAM TROWBRIDGE

PUT THIS ON, PLEASE
New & Selected Poems
by William Trowbridge

208 pages
978-1-59709-966-0 • Tradepaper • 19.95

William Trowbridge's *Put This On, Please: New and Selected Poems* contains work from all five of his full collections, as well as a group of new poems that continues his often seriocomic account of human foibles, vices, and wonders. In these reader-friendly poems, Trowbridge draws often from classic films and other elements of popular culture—from Buster Keaton to Chuck Berry, from King Kong to Wile E. Coyote. Trowbridge is not squeamish about exploring the darker side of humanity, as in poems about the Kiss of Death, delivered by Michael Corleone in The Godfather II, or Charles Starkweather, mass murderer and the last person to die in the Nebraska electric chair. Capping off the book, a group of new poems takes a fresh look at old themes, sounding deepened notes of both melancholy and celebration. Throughout, Trowbridge makes a strong case for laughter as the only appropriate response to our post-post-modern condition.

Praise for *Put This On, Please*

"To call William Trowbridge a plain-spoken poet is accurate and one of his great virtues: he is unafraid of being understood. He is also a master of metaphor and, one never doubts the honesty of his poems, his voice. His poems speak, oh they speak! What he does is very hard to do and he does it brilliantly."

—Thomas Lux

"[Trowbridge] easily captures the rhythm and hum of everyday life. Discussing Buster Keaton or Chuck Berry, King Kong or Wile E. Coyote, Trowbridge wittily explores our need for fulfillment and our failures in finding it. Trowbridge succeeds—making readers smile while plumbing something deeper than a giggle."

—Jonathan Shipley, *Shelf Awareness*

Available from the Chicago Distribution Center
To place an order: (800) 621-2736 / www.redhen.org

ALMOST RAIN
SIMON PERCHIK

From earlier books:

"At Corinth, two temples stood next to one another: one to violence and one to necessity. Mr. Perchik's poems attend both temples, and are often terrifying compressions of the violence in simple daily acts." **Paul Blackburn**

"So much of what Perchik does include (but leaves at the heart level) is this important thing and I always hear it, as he knows, in what he does." **Charles Olson**

"Much like William Bronk or Jack Spicer, Perchik is a poet's poet…of deep, brooding poems that reflect and encompass an amazing spectrum of human experience…refracted through the eyes and mind of an exceptionally gifted poet." **Rain Taxi**

"This is certainly no derivative collection, but rather a unique meditation on the orogeny of a soul." **Boston Review**

"Perchik is the most widely published unknown poet in America ... who may well be our era's Emily Dickinson. **Library Journal**

"What is always clear is that this is a complex, lyrical vision of the commonplace. Even a meager narrative is hardly worth noticing, finally, in the midst of these exquisite imaginings. It is the constant struggle in this process which empowers his poetry and provides tension to his lyric." **Mid-American Review**

"…working close to the deeper sources of poetry, in modes reflecting individuality and technical determination, Mr. Perchik is the most original..." **Poetry**

"Let others jockey for position. Perchik's poems are obdurant and honest and will reach those who need them most." **James Tate**

"Simon Perchik's extraordinary lyric talent is one of the best kept secrets in contemporary American poetry. His surreal leaps orchestrate very personal material into archetypal configurations that approach transcendence."**Edward Butscher**

Mr. Perchik's poetry has been published in Partisan Review,
The Nation, Poetry and The New Yorker.

For more information on Simon Perchik, go to
www.simonperchik.com

River Otter Press
PO Box 211664   St. Paul, MN 55121
RiverOtterPress@gmail.com
Soft Cover $12.99 available on Amazon.com
Hard Cover $29.99 available at RiverOtterPress@gmail.com

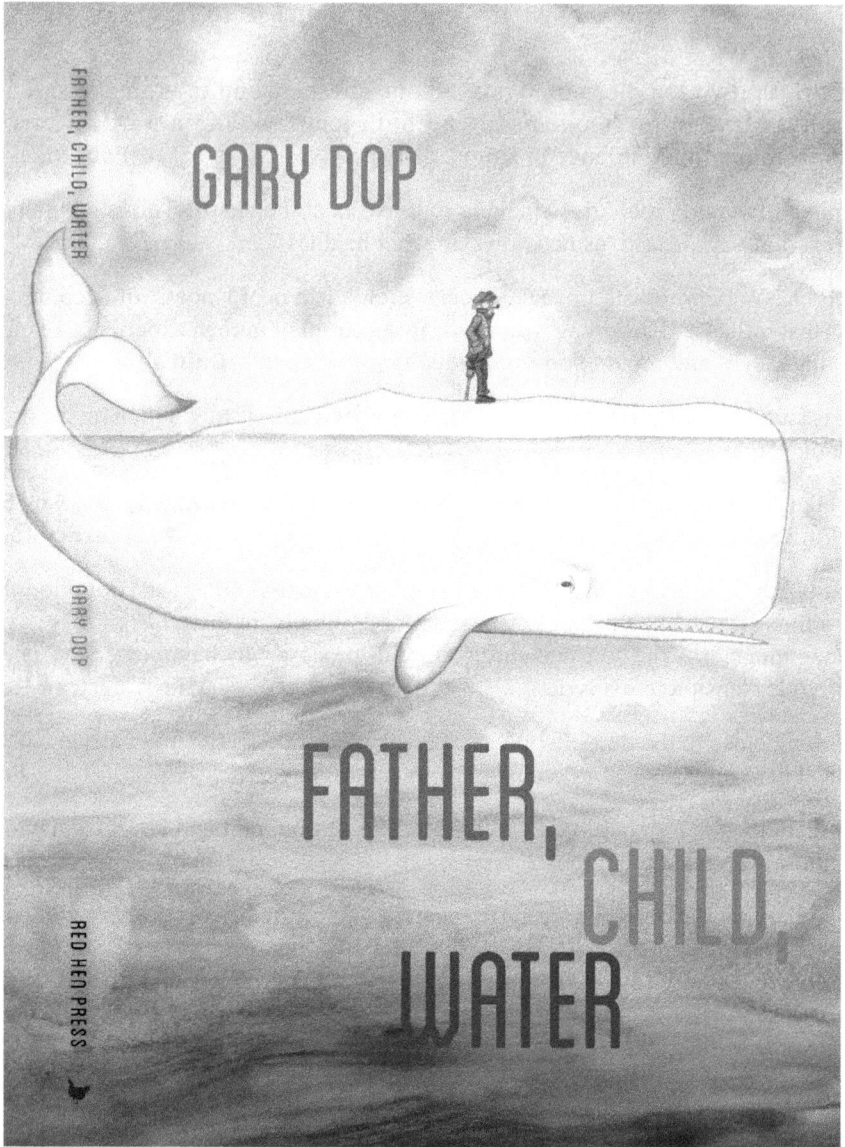

GARY DOP

FATHER, CHILD, WATER

RED HEN PRESS

"Like a spoiler come to destroy the church's summer potluck, the institutions of fathering (national, religious, familial) are compassionately questioned here, as Dop navigates patriarchal inheritances of violence and war, while defining his own role as a nurturing father—one seeking to protect and empower his own daughters from the brutal codes of obligatory masculinity."
—LEE ANN RORIPAUGH

SPRING

SUMMER

FALL

THE
BLUESHIFT
JOURNAL

PROSE

POETRY

ART

The Crafty Poet
A Portable Workshop

by
Diane Lockward

Wind Publications

A poetry tutorial to inform and inspire poets. Includes model poems and prompts, writing tips, and interviews with poets. Geared for experienced poets as well as those just getting started. Ideal for individual use at home or group use in the classroom or workshop.

101 Contributors Including

Kim Addonizio
Ellen Bass
Jan Beatty
Kathryn Stripling Byer
Kelly Cherry
Marilyn Hacker
Jane Hirshfield
Dorianne Laux
Sydney Lea
Jeffrey Levine
Wesley McNair
Alicia Ostriker
Linda Pastan
Stanley Plumly
Lee Upton
Baron Wormser

. . . an important new resource for poets—those who are just beginning as well as the more seasoned poet.—Susan Rich

. . . a spectacular array of model poems and information from poets on how they see the craft. It will get you writing and will keep you writing.—Sheila Bender

. . . a *must* for teachers of poetry. . .What a way to ease our students into finding their own toolboxes.—Grace Cavalieri

Wind Publications, 600 Overbrook Drive, Nicholasville, KY 40356
ISBN: 978-1936138623 Price: $20
www.windpub.com   books@windpub.com
Available at Amazon, B&N, or your favorite bookstore

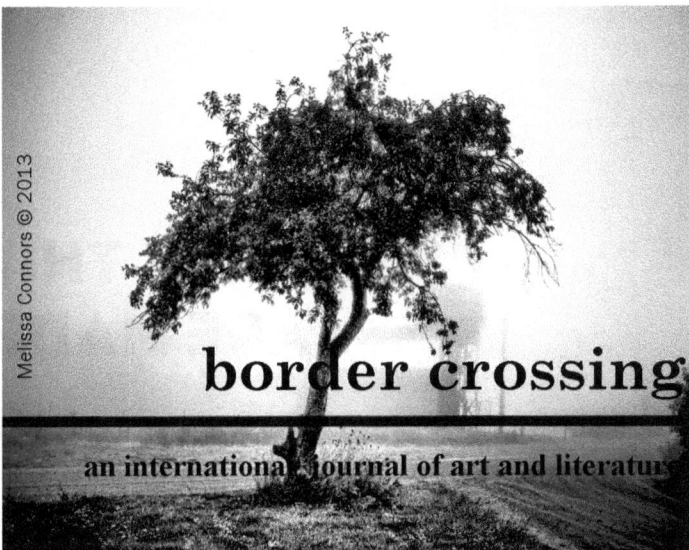

Melissa Connors © 2013

border crossing

an international journal of art and literature

CALL FOR SUBMISSIONS

Housed at Lake Superior State University on the border of the U.S. and Canada, we seek the best fiction, nonfiction, poetry, and hybrid work by emerging and established authors in both countries and abroad. Annual reading period opens September 15 and closes February 1. Online submissions. No reading fee. Submit writing that crosses boundaries in genre or geography, and voices that aren't often heard in mainstream publications. To see what we mean by this, order a copy of our latest issue. Beginning with vol. 5, we are an online journal, and we will run paid features of selected authors. Visit our website to learn more.

www.lssu.edu/bc

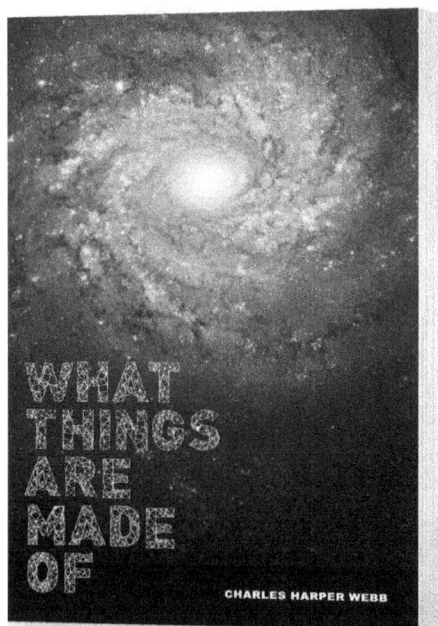

WHAT THINGS ARE MADE OF

Charles Harper Webb

104 pp. ▪ Paper ▪ $15.95

ISBN 978-0-8229-6229-8

"Webb displays such a wonderfully quirky, idiosyncratic voice, whether writing about oil-slicked, doomed penguins or puppy love. His poems careen between wild hyperboles, the irony of looking back at youthful indiscretions and unrequited or disappointed love, to the joy he feels with his beloved small son and wife, and his love of old rock bands like the Stones or Led Zeppelin. But there's always something interesting, fascinating in this collection, something that makes us read and keep turning the pages, to see what new and deliriously strange take he'll have on the things of this world."

—Chamber Four

SUGAR HOUSE REVIEW

AN INDEPENDENT POETRY MAGAZINE

RECENT CONTRIBUTORS

Dan Beachy-Quick	Claudia Keelan	Paul Muldoon	Patricia Smith
Anne Caston	William Kloefkorn	Carl Phillips	Janet Sylvester
Kate Greenstreet	Jeffrey McDaniel	Donald Revell	Pimone Triplett
Major Jackson	Campbell McGrath	Natasha Sajé	Joshua Marie Wilkinson

Work from our pages has been included in *Verse Daily*, *Poetry Daily*, and *Pushcart Prize: Best of the Small Presses,* 2015, 2014, 2013, and 2011.

GET YOUR SUGAR FIX

One Year: $12   Two Years: $22   PDF Version: $2

SUBMIT, SUBSCRIBE, PASS US ALONG.

www.SugarHouseReview.com

NESTUARY

MOLLY SUTTON KIEFER

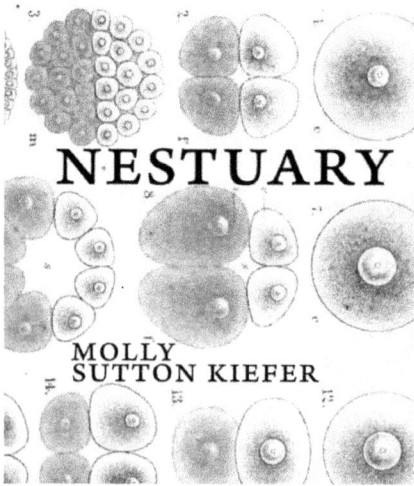

"This book-length lyric essay provides gently incisive scrutiny of the processes (biological, social, psychological, cultural, even economic) of planned motherhood. Kiefer employs verse, memoir, reportage, and a quietly tenacious prose narrative to style a private moment-by-moment mosaic of experience. Discussions of gender and privilege blend seamlessly with larger, core interrogations of the body itself –that which perseveres and triumphs, that which fails in myriad ways and despairs helplessly of those failures –that which creates and that which betrays itself."

-- Arielle Greenberg

Available on Amazon, bn.com, Powells.com, SPD books, and on Ricochet Editions' website. For more information, see www.mollysuttonkiefer.com

TINDERBOX
POETRY JOURNAL

www.tinderboxpoetry.com

Read work from DA Powell, Carmen Gimenez Smith, Amy Gerstler, Ed Skoog, Leslie Harrison, and Rachel Richardson, among others. We read year-round and we're interested in a range of aesthetics, including the lyric essay. We also accept conversations and essays on poetics. Watch the website for our first annual contest this coming spring!

Lullabies
Are
Barbed
Wire
Nations

Poems by
NANDINI DHAR